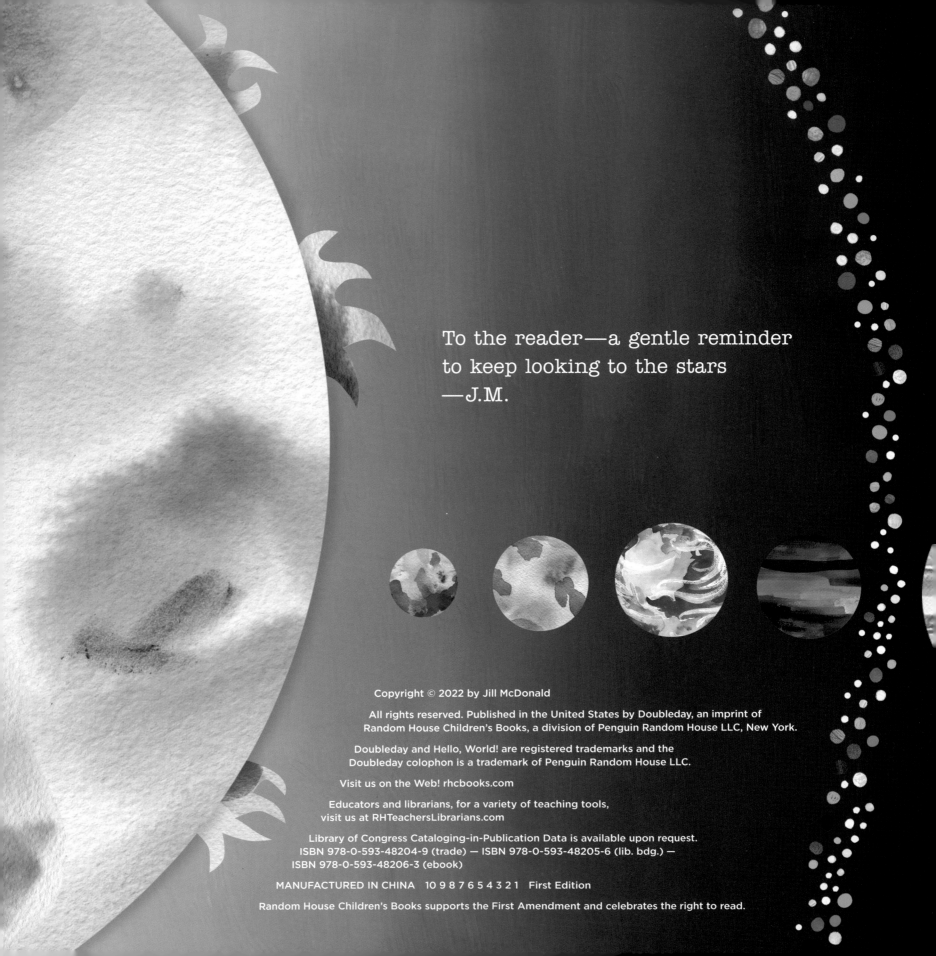

To the reader—a gentle reminder
to keep looking to the stars
—J.M.

All rights reserved. Published in the United States by Doubleday, an imprint of
Random House Children's Books, a division of Penguin Random House LLC, New York.

Doubleday and Hello, World! are registered trademarks and the
Doubleday colophon is a trademark of Penguin Random House LLC.

Visit us on the Web! rhcbooks.com

Educators and librarians, for a variety of teaching tools,
visit us at RHTeachersLibrarians.com

Library of Congress Cataloging-in-Publication Data is available upon request.
ISBN 978-0-593-48204-9 (trade) — ISBN 978-0-593-48205-6 (lib. bdg.) —
ISBN 978-0-593-48206-3 (ebook)

MANUFACTURED IN CHINA   10 9 8 7 6 5 4 3 2 1   First Edition

HELLO, WORLD!®

KIDS' GUIDES

# Exploring the SOLAR System

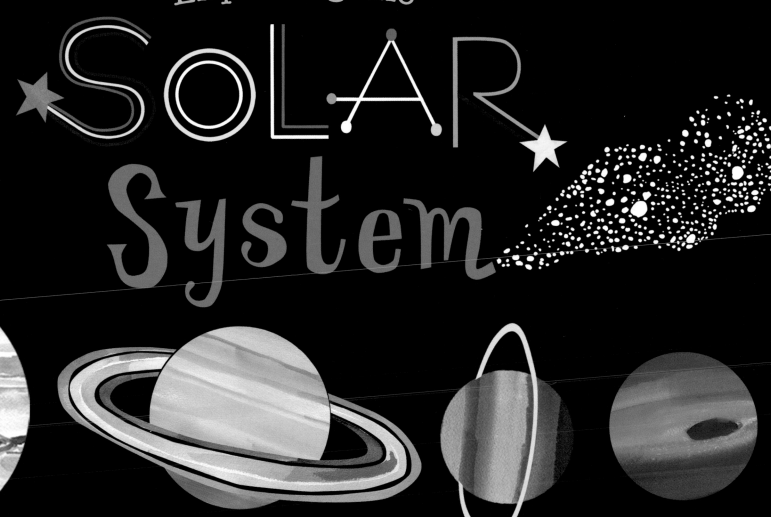

## Jill McDonald

Doubleday Books for Young Readers

Welcome to the universe.
Population: you!

The universe is everything that exists, in all of space and all of time.

The universe has billions of galaxies. A galaxy is a huge collection of stars, solar systems, gas, and dust. Our galaxy is called the Milky Way.

Think of our solar system as our neighborhood. The sun is at the center, and eight planets travel around it, plus moons, dwarf planets, asteroids, comets, and meteoroids.

\* Gravity is a pulling force. Without gravity, we would float away. Because the sun is the biggest thing in our solar system, its gravity pulls everything toward it.

Humans have always kept their eyes on the stars. Now we also have technology—such as rockets, telescopes, satellites, rovers, and probes—to help us see much farther.

Ready to blast off and explore?

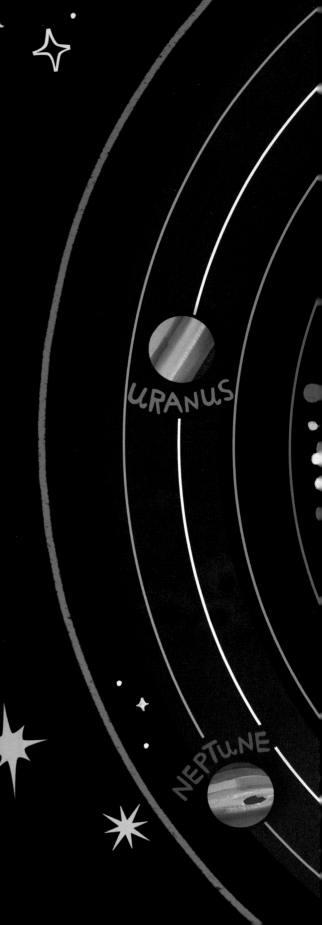

URANUS

NEPTUNE

## The Sun

is a massive star of glowing gases. It's the closest star to Earth, but it's still very far away: ninety-three million miles (150 million km)! Animals and plants can live on Earth because of the sun's light and warmth.

The sun and Earth are why we have seasons. Earth orbits around the sun once a year. Earth rotates on a tilted axis, so different parts of Earth receive the sun's most direct rays at different times.

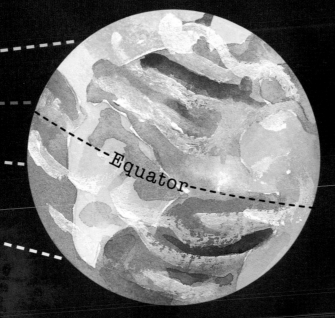

* The top half of Earth is called the Northern Hemisphere.

Equator

* The bottom half is the Southern Hemisphere.

When the North Pole tilts toward the sun, it's summer in the top half of Earth. At the same time, it's winter in the bottom half of Earth. When the South Pole tilts toward the sun, it's winter in the top half of Earth and summer in the bottom half.

# The STATS

Size (around the equator):
2.7 million miles
(4.4 million km)

Average temperature (core):
27 million°F
(15 million°C)

Average temperature (surface):
10,000°F (5,500°C)

Made of:
92.1% hydrogen, 7.8% helium, 0.1% other elements

Type of star:
Yellow dwarf star

# QUESTION

What do you like best about a sunrise in the morning? What do you like best about a sunset at night?

# Mercury

is the smallest planet in the solar system, just a little bigger than Earth's moon. It's also the closest planet to the sun.

If you visited Mercury, the daylight would be seven times brighter than on Earth. Bring your sunglasses!

But at night, Mercury is cold! Mercury doesn't have an atmosphere, a layer of gas that surrounds a planet. Because of this, the daytime heat escapes.

Mercury wins the award for most craters of any planet in the solar system. It has been bombarded by LOTS of asteroids and comets. **YIKES!**

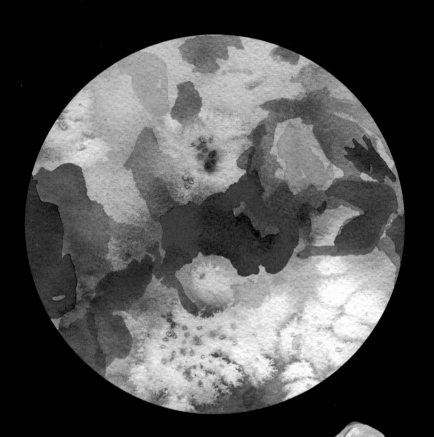

1

SUN

MERCURY

VENUS

EARTH

JUPITER

Mercury does not have a moon. Why? Because Mercury is so close to the sun, the sun's strong gravity would pull a moon out of its orbit.

A day is how long it takes a planet to make one full rotation.

A year is how long it takes a planet to orbit around the sun.

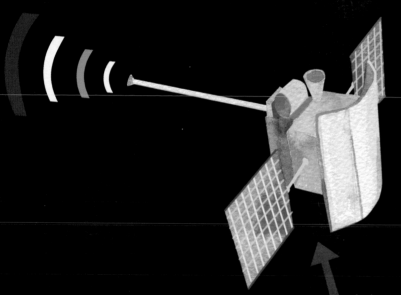

MESSENGER

\* In 2012, NASA's spacecraft Messenger discovered frozen water at Mercury's North Pole.

SATURN

URANUS

NEPTUNE

# The STATS

**Size (around the equator):**
9,525 miles (15,329 km)

**Distance from the sun:**
36 million miles (58 million km)

**Average temperature:**
800°F (430°C) (day),
−290°F (−180°C) (night)

**Length of a day:**
1,408 hours

**Length of a year (in Earth days):**
88 days

**Number of moons:** 0

# QUESTION

**Would you rather live on a hot planet or a cold planet?**

# Venus

is Earth's closest neighbor and the brightest object in the sky after the sun and moon. You can see Venus from Earth without a telescope!

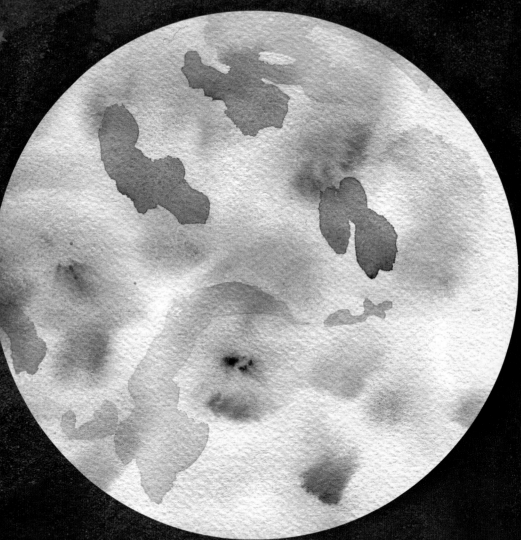

SuN

MERCURY

2

VENUS

EARTH

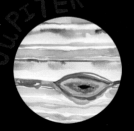
JUPITER

Life on Venus would be hard! This planet is covered in thick clouds of poisonous sulfuric acid that smell like rotten eggs!

Venus isn't the closest planet to the sun, but it is the hottest. The clouds trap heat on the surface, making it very hot. The temperature is so high, some metals would melt into liquid.

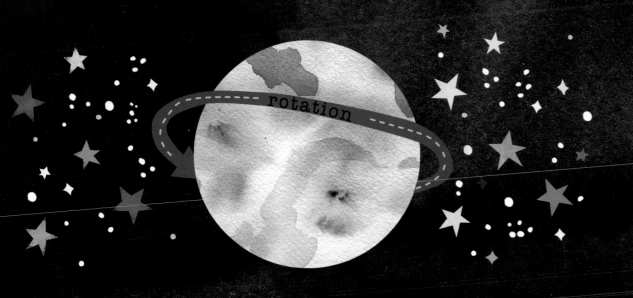

rotation

Venus and Uranus are the only two planets in the solar system that rotate the opposite direction of Earth, so the sun rises in the west and sets in the east.

\* Venus has more volcanoes than any other planet in the solar system.

SATURN

URANUS

NEPTUNE

rotation

# The STATS

**Size (around the equator):**
23,627 miles (38,025 km)

**Distance from the sun:**
67.2 million miles
(108.2 million km)

**Average temperature:**
880°F (471°C)

**Length of a day:**
5,832 hours

**Length of a year
(in Earth days):**
225 days

**Number of moons: 0**

# QUESTION

One day on Venus lasts as long as 243 days on Earth! What would you do on such a long day?

# Earth

is the third planet from the sun and the one we call home. It has four main layers: the inner core, the outer core, the mantle, and the crust. Almost three-quarters of Earth is covered in water.

* Earth is the only planet in our solar system where life is known to exist.

3
EARTH

SUN  MERCURY  VENUS   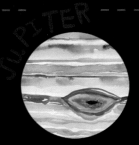 JUPITER

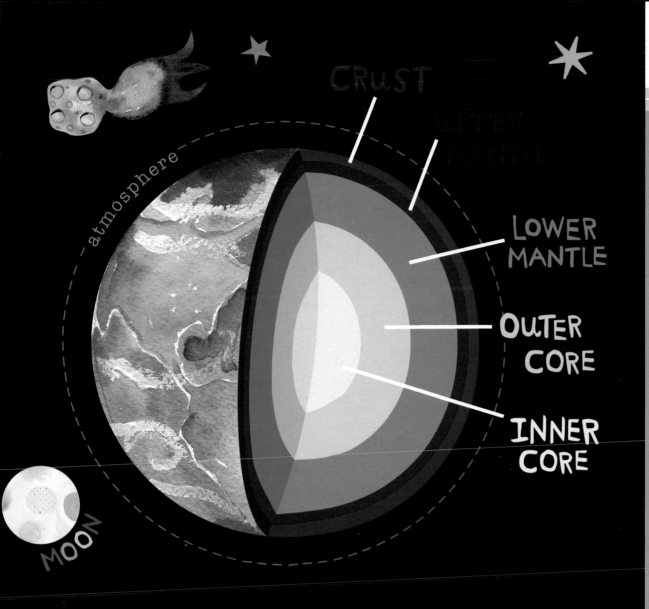

CRUST

UPPER MANTLE

LOWER MANTLE

OUTER CORE

INNER CORE

atmosphere

MOON

Earth's atmosphere is a layer of gas that wraps around our planet like a blanket. It gives us the oxygen we breathe and keeps us warm. It also acts as a protective shield. When meteoroids approach Earth, they usually burn up before they have a chance to reach the surface.

SATURN

URANUS

NEPTUNE

## QUESTION

What's your favorite thing about living on Earth?

**Mars** is known as the Red Planet. Its surface contains iron, which rusts and gives Mars its red color.

OLYMPUS MONS

Two small moons orbit Mars: Phobos and Deimos. They aren't round like Earth's moon. They are shaped like lumpy potatoes.

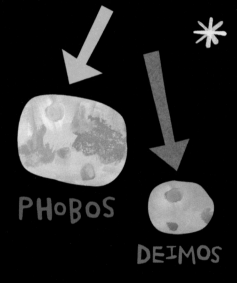

PHOBOS

DEIMOS

In thirty to fifty million years (a really long time), Phobos will collide with Mars or be torn into rubble, creating a ring around the planet.

4

SUN

MERCURY

VENUS

EARTH

JUPITER

Ready for a climbing adventure? Mars is home to Olympus Mons, the tallest mountain in the solar system. It is almost three times as high as Mount Everest, Earth's tallest mountain.

*Olympus Mons is a volcano, created by lava flowing up from the ground.

Humans have never been to Mars, but spacecrafts have, starting in 1971. In 2021, a rover, *Perseverance*, and a helicopter, *Ingenuity*, landed there after a seven-month voyage. The helicopter collects information that a rover on the ground can't see. What a team!

*Ingenuity* is the first helicopter to fly over another planet.

SATURN
URANUS
NEPTUNE

# The STATS

**Size (around the equator):**
13,233 miles (21,297 km)

**Distance from the sun:**
141.6 million miles
(227.9 million km)

**Average temperature:**
–20°F (–28°C)

**Length of a day:**
25 hours

**Length of a year
(in Earth days):**
687 days

**Number of moons: 2**
●●

# QUESTION

**What would you bring with you on your Mars mission?**

# Jupiter

is the oldest and largest planet in our solar system, over twice as massive as all the other planets combined!

You couldn't land on Jupiter. This stripy planet is a gas giant, made up mostly of hydrogen and helium, and doesn't have a hard surface like Earth. Scientists don't know if Jupiter has a solid core.

\* Saturn is also a gas giant.

SUN

MERCURY

VENUS

EARTH

JUPITER

5

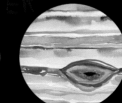

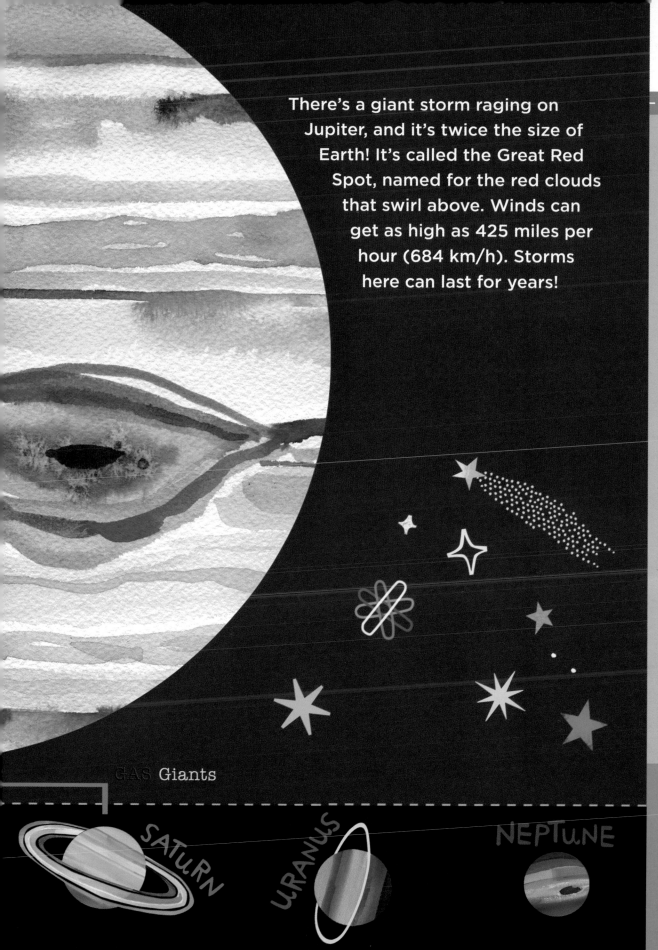

There's a giant storm raging on Jupiter, and it's twice the size of Earth! It's called the Great Red Spot, named for the red clouds that swirl above. Winds can get as high as 425 miles per hour (684 km/h). Storms here can last for years!

GAS Giants

SATURN    URANUS    NEPTUNE

**Size (around the equator):**
272,946 miles (439,264 km)

**Distance from the sun:**
483.8 million miles
(778.6 million km)

**Average temperature:**
–162°F (–108°C)

**Length of a day:**
10 hours

**Length of a year
(in Earth days):**
4,333 days

**Number of moons: 79
(53 confirmed, 26 unconfirmed)**

# QUESTION

**What color clouds would you
like to have on your planet?**

# Saturn

is famous for its rings. The rings aren't solid. They're made up of rock and ice. Scientists think these pieces might have been asteroids, comets, or moons that were broken up by Saturn's strong gravity.

* Saturn is squished! The planet spins so fast, it gets flattened out.

CASSINI
spacecraft

probe

SUN

MERCURY

VENUS

EARTH

JUPITER

In 2004, the *Cassini* spacecraft arrived at Saturn, along with its probe, *Huygens*. *Cassini-Huygens* was the first mission to orbit Saturn. It took seven years to arrive from Earth and stayed for thirteen years, gathering photos and important new information about this planet.

*Cassini* discovered that Enceladus, one of Saturn's eighty-two moons, has geysers that shoot out ice and gas—the possible building blocks of life!

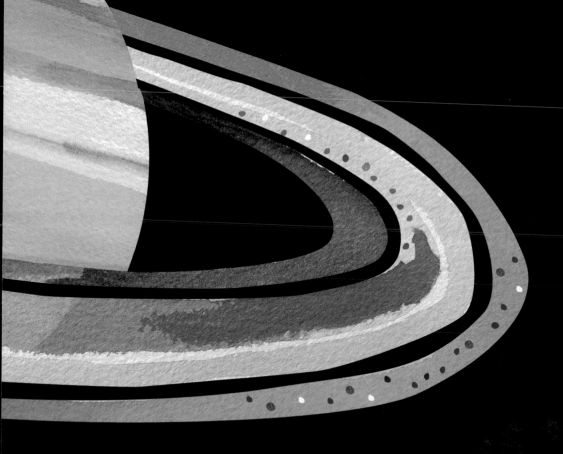

SATURN

6

URANUS

NEPTUNE

# Uranus

is the coldest planet in the solar system. This ice giant is nearly four times the size of Earth. Uranus is blue because of the methane in its atmosphere.

Uranus has a surprise: It rotates on its side!

All the other planets spin horizontally like tops. Scientists think an object the size of Earth might have hit it, causing it to tilt.

Because of the way Uranus spins and the position of the sun's rays, winter and summer on Uranus each last twenty-one Earth years!

SUN

MERCURY

VENUS

EARTH

MARS

JUPITER

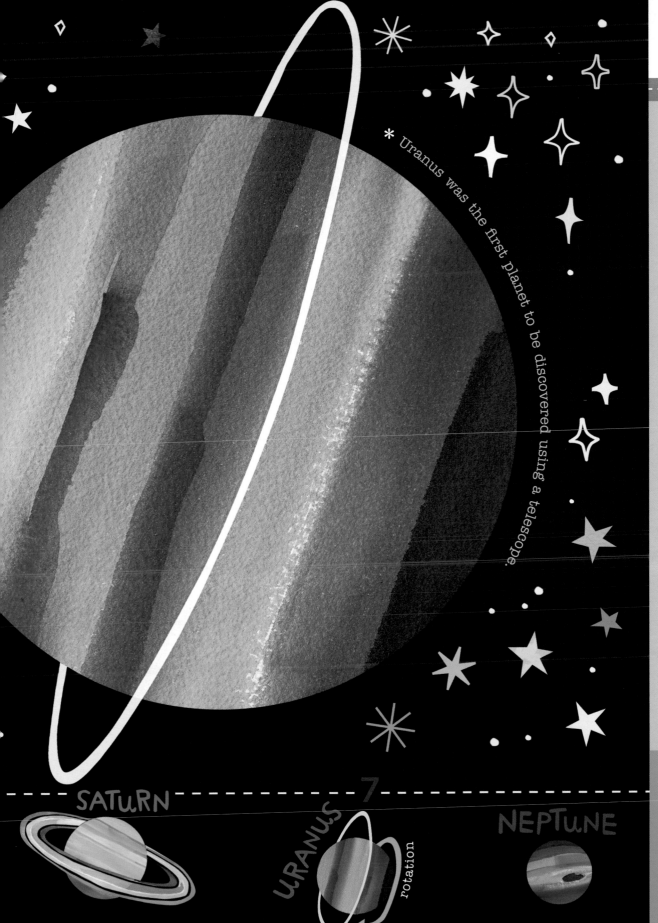

* Uranus was the first planet to be discovered using a telescope.

SATURN

URANUS 7

rotation

NEPTUNE

**Size (around the equator):**
99,018 miles (159,354 km)

**Distance from the sun:**
1.8 billion miles
(2.9 billion km)

**Average temperature:**
–320°F (–195°C)

**Length of a day:**
17 hours

**Length of a year
(in Earth days):**
30,687 days

**Number of moons: 27**
●●●●●●●●●●●●
●●●●●●●●●●●●
●●●

## QUESTION

If you were a planet, what
would you name your moons?

# Neptune

is the farthest planet in our solar system from the sun. Because it's so far away, it doesn't get many visitors. *Voyager 2* is the only spacecraft to have studied Neptune up close.

Like Uranus, Neptune is an ice giant and is blue because of the methane gas in its atmosphere.

\* In 2018, the Hubble Space Telescope discovered a storm on Neptune that was wider than the Atlantic Ocean.

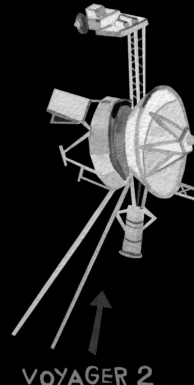

VOYAGER 2

Neptune is the windiest planet in the solar system. Winds can reach 1,200 miles per hour (1,931 km/h). The strongest wind ever recorded on Earth was 253 miles per hour (407 km/h).

Neptune is also dark! It is so far away from the sun, it doesn't get the same sunlight we do. The sunlight on Earth is about 900 times brighter.

SUN

MERCURY

VENUS

EARTH

MARS

JUPITER

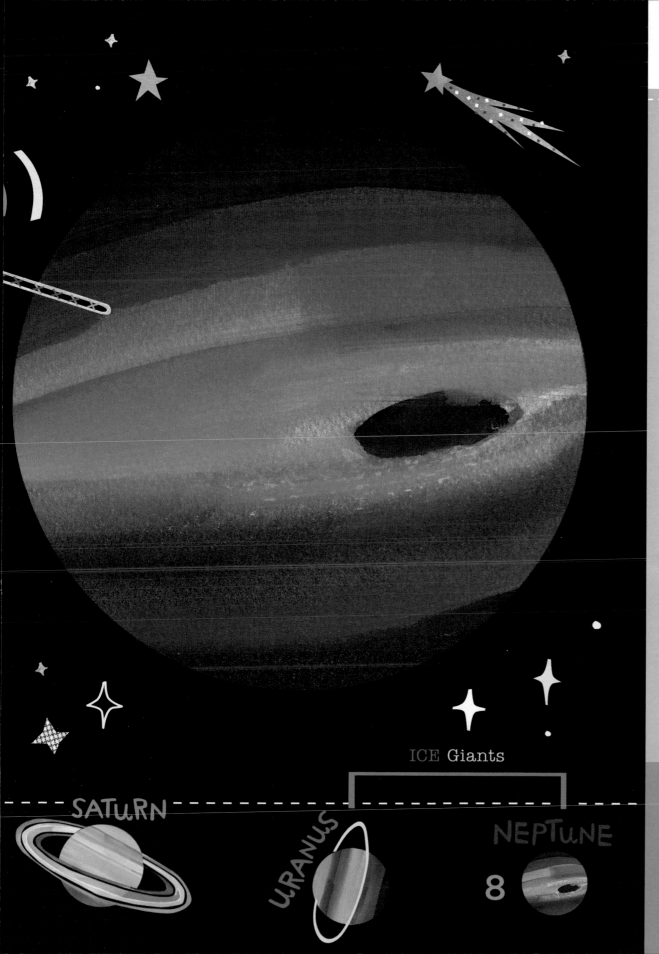

# The STATS

**Size (around the equator):**
96,129 miles (154,705 km)

**Distance from the sun:**
2.8 billion miles
(4.5 billion km)

**Average temperature:**
–331°F (–201°C)

**Length of a day:**
16 hours

**Length of a year
(in Earth days):**
60,190 days

**Number of moons: 14**

ICE Giants

SATURN

URANUS

NEPTUNE

8

# QUESTION

What would you bring with you
to a planet that's always dark?

There once was a planet named Pluto.

It was the farthest planet from the sun. But in 2006, that changed.
Scientists decided Pluto was no longer a planet, but a dwarf planet instead.

There are three rules for being a planet, and Pluto only meets the first two:
1. A planet is in orbit around the sun.
2. It is round.
3. It has so much gravitational force, there are no other bodies of a
   similar size in its region.

But don't feel sorry for Pluto! It has some fascinating features. Pluto has
mountains close to the size of Earth's Rocky Mountains and a big icy area
that's shaped like a heart.

\* Pluto was named by an eleven-year-old girl! In 1930, Venetia Burney had the idea
  of naming it after the Roman god of the underworld. Her grandfather brought
  the name to the astronomer who had discovered the planet, and he liked it!

Eris

Ceres

Makemake

Scientists think there could be many dwarf planets in our solar system. So far, they've found five: Pluto, Ceres, Eris, Makemake, and Haumea.

Haumea

How do we know so much about planets and stars that are so far away?

Scientific agencies such as NASA in the United States are always developing new technology to allow humans and machines to travel farther into space.

✳ NASA stands for National Aeronautics and Space Administration.

Humans first landed on Earth's moon in 1969 and stayed for just over twenty-one hours. Now there are people who live and work in space for months at a time.

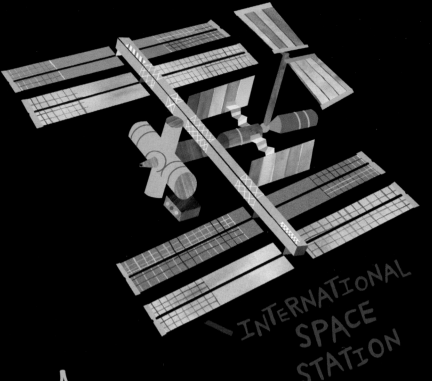

INTERNATIONAL SPACE STATION

The International Space Station is a research lab that orbits Earth. Astronauts from around the world share the space station to conduct experiments.

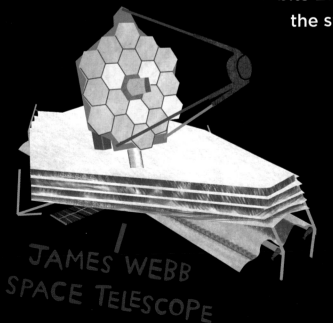

JAMES WEBB SPACE TELESCOPE

SATELLITE

Not every mission requires an astronaut. Space probes, satellites, and telescopes travel through space without humans on board. These machines collect scientific information to send back to Earth.

You can do your own research at home. A telescope lets you study stars, planets, and galaxies. Or you can simply look up at the sky tonight and let your imagination and curiosity take you far away.

**What do you see?**